Swimming
with the
Elephants
and other adventures

*Discoveries for the
curious traveller's bucket list*

Anne Louise O'Connell

Swimming with the Elephants
Copyright © 2018 Anne Louise O'Connell
Second edition, 2025

All rights reserved under international copyright conventions. No part of this publication may be reproduced, stored in or introduced into a retrieval system, or transmitted in any form, or by any means, without the prior written permission of the author.

Published by

Halifax, NS, Canada
www.ocpublishing.ca

First published in 2015

Interior book design by David W. Edelstein

ISBN 978-1-989833-33-9 (Paperback edition)
ISBN 978-1-989833-51-3 (GCA certified eBook edition)

This one's for M.T.

CONTENTS

Introduction *1*

1. Koh Chang, Thailand -
   Swimming with the Elephants 3

2. Dubai to Thailand - The Transition 7

3. Island Living - Not so Boring After All 11

4. Songkran - The Biggest Water Fight in the World .. 17

5. Phuket Vegetarian Festival 21

6. Exploring the Outskirts 25

7. Fun Phuket Tourist Traps 29

8. Motorbike Mash-up 35

9. Wandering Around any 'Old Town' 39

10. You Can EAT That? 43

11. The Thailand De-tox 47

12. Thailand Island Hopping in Style 59

13. Jakarta, Indonesia........................... 65

14. Exploring Malaysia – Sights, Sounds & Smells ... 69

15. Petra, Jordan - Rescued by a Bedouin........... 77

16. South Africa - Kapama Game Park 91

17. The Floating Islands of Peru................... 97

18. Bare Boating BVI Style 101

19. Sailing the Greek Isles....................... 105

20. Exploring the Greek Island of Hydra........... 111

21. Sailing St. Lucia to Martinique................. 115

About the Author *119*

INTRODUCTION

I want to thank my mom, fondly known as Mother Theresa, or M.T. for short, who inspired this collection. She always loved to hear about my travel tales and I never held anything back... she wanted to hear the good, the bad and even the ugly! Her favourite story was the one where I swam with the elephants in Koh Chang, Thailand, which is the first story in the book. One day we were chatting on the phone and she made a proclamation, "I know what your next book should be called." I replied, "Oh Yeah? What's that?" She said, "Swimming with the Elephants and other Adventures." She had told me about a hundred times, "You should write a book about all your adventures." I agreed it wouldn't be that hard, since I had written several articles and blogs so it would really be a matter of compiling them and doing a bit of an edit. Her enthusiasm caught on and I promised I would do it. And, I kind of liked the title. So, after a few pauses to launch other books, it was published, originally in 2015, and the ebook more recently, in 2024.

CHAPTER 1

Koh Chang, Thailand – Swimming with the Elephants

After moving to Dubai, we were planning our first visit to Thailand and some good friends recommended the island of Koh Chang (Elephant Island). It is Thailand's second largest island and there are plenty of beaches to laze on, which is one of my favourite things to do, along with lots of hiking. Like many adventure travellers we seek out the less crowded places and avoid heavily populated tourist towns. As Phuket, Koh Samui and Koh Phangna (of full moon party fame) become more hectic, especially in high season, Koh Chang seemed to have kept its appeal as a more remote and not so commercialized destination.

One afternoon after arriving on the island, we were looking for something different to do and discovered that there were numerous tour operators in Thailand that will take visitors on elephant rides. Of course, we wanted to avoid the crowds so we found the tiny enterprise of Ban Kwan Chang, hidden in the hills of Koh Chang at Ban Klong Son Village. Finding this remote little gem added a new twist to our adventure.

We were the only ones there on that day. Our elephants (and their handlers) took us on a long, pleasant, leisurely plod through the jungle. They stopped regularly to munch on various leafy green delights while the handlers pointed out indigenous flora and fauna. According to the book, *The National Parks of Thailand*, there are more than 500 species of trees, over 1,000 varieties of orchids, 900 recorded species of birds and 1,200 types of butterflies to entertain trekkers along the trail.

The jungle trail led us to a beautiful river and the ride continued alongside the river. As it widened, the handlers gave an order to the elephants and our entourage paused on the river's edge. At first glance, there seemed to be nothing around but rocks and trees but a closer inspection showed a raised wooden platform jutting out over a pool at the end.

The handlers gracefully guided the elephants up to the platform where we hopped off. The elephants were then liberated from the heavy wooden and metal chairs on which we had been perched. We climbed on again but bareback this time and the elephants happily waded into the deeper pool ready for a swim and a bath, spraying each other and us in turn.

At one point my elephant, Som-O, sunk deep into the water so I floated off her back; she resurfaced right beside me. I held on to her ear and looked into her eye. It was a beautiful deep, coffee bean brown, with two-inch long eyelashes. The joy of playing in the water emanated from her as I whispered in her ear, thanking her for my ride. I felt a soft puff of wind against the side of my head. I looked around and saw that her trunk was curved up out of the water and she was sniffing and nuzzling me! It was a moment of connection with a rather large animal that I will never forget.

After the refreshing plunge in the pool, we enjoyed a pleasant ride back along the dusty trail through the jungle.

Koh Chang is sparsely populated with quaint towns dotting the coastline mostly on the western and southern parts of the island. The main livelihood is fishing. The interior, mountainous, uninhabited part of the island is predominantly virgin rainforest. The tallest mountain peaks at 744 metres above sea level. The island, located eight kilometres off the coast of Trat on the East side of the Gulf of Thailand, is part of an archipelago of islands, which includes Koh Kut, Koh Mak and Koh Kradat.

I highly recommend a visit to Koh Chang and, if

you do, check out the elephant rides and my other favourite place on the island, Bang Bao Pier. Maybe even stay there. You can channel your inner hippy!

CHAPTER 2

Dubai to Thailand – The Transition

As I massacred a spider as big as my hand with a broom that was thankfully close by, I couldn't help but think to myself, *they didn't come that big in Dubai*. But here I was in Thailand and that's one of the things that I adjusted to (umm, not really) after moving to the beautiful island of Phuket.

The transition went relatively smoothly I loved my new life in Thailand, surrounded by beautiful plants and flowers and listening to the birds singing happily every morning as I drank my morning coffee on the balcony. The beach was a five-minute drive away and the food was glorious. I constantly marvelled at the burst of flavours in each and every bite. Fruits and vegetables were crisper and herbs and spices more pungent.

But... (You knew there was a but somewhere in there, didn't you?), there are bumps along the road of every change in life. Sometimes you can't just swerve around them. If you ignore them, eventually you'll hit one straight on and wind up scraping or denting your undercarriage.

The Change

Making transitions can be tough and change, even when we choose it, takes some time to smooth out. The change of moving to Thailand was exhilarating, as we had been talking about it for a couple of years. However, there were other changes afoot. Right at that juncture, I was in the midst of *"THE CHANGE."* You know, night sweats, hot flashes, mental pauses and paranoia. Combine that with convincing clients that I could still work for them even from Thailand and saying goodbye to the amazing friends I had made, it was just a bit rough and there were some teary moments. Fortunately, with Facebook and Skype it's easier to keep that promise to stay in touch, and we have.

Settling into Expat Life in Thailand

I read tons of advice from others who had made the transition several times (and had even written a book myself about getting settled in Dubai) and they say it's not good to keep one foot in your past and one in your present. For the first several months I kept telling myself, "Get out there and meet people! Join groups, have dinner parties, strike-up conversations with strangers." I know the drill. But I happily isolated myself in my office busily working away on an assortment of writing projects. Oh, every once in a while, I half-heartedly did a Google search for forums or networking groups in Thailand but most times I ran into a cyber wall as the majority of groups were in Bangkok. It's not that far by airplane but too far to join in with any type of frequency. So, I dove deeper into my cave (no, it's not just men who do that... admit it girls... we do it too). I would surface periodically to go for a motorbike ride, get a massage on the beach or visit with one of my Thai girlfriends down the road. But, the ever-elusive expat community just wasn't knocking down my door like it did in Dubai, usually armed with a nice bottle of Cabernet.

Patience is a Virtue

Then... I found a networking group called ChickyNet (which does not exist anymore but was a godsend for me at the time). It was totally by accident and I have to believe it waited until I was ready for it. Some of the best experiences in life are the ones that are unexpected. Like the email I got from a neighbour from back home who said a friend was going to be in Phuket on business and could she get in touch?

Of course, I said yes. I wound up joining her on a reconnaissance mission scoping out anchorages and dive spots around the out islands, had a wonderful day and the wife of the owner of the boat introduced me to this expat woman's forum in Thailand, with a group in Phuket. There's no way I could have planned that! I joined in on a few events and met an Aussie gal who became my best friend in Phuket. There was no writing group though, so I did what I do... I started one up!

So, the secret to smoothing out the transition and handling change really boils down to being open to new experiences, which I've always been, and just rolling with it, which I usually do. I will always have a toehold in my past because some things (and people) are worth hanging on to.

CHAPTER 3

Island Living – Not so Boring After All

Pinch me! I thought to myself as I realized I was really living on an island. It had been a dream of mine for a very long time. I actually grew up in a small province of Canada called Nova Scotia that is almost an island except for the swatch of land connecting it to New Brunswick. For the first half of my life, I was never far away from the Atlantic Ocean... that, coupled with being a water sign, clinched it for me. I've always been drawn to any large body of water, only as I got older, it had to be in warmer climes.

During our working lives, so many of us Canadians dream of digging our toes in the sand, sipping on our cold beverage of choice and watching the sun dip lazily into the sea at the end of the day. Then reality takes over and you're slogging away again at your desk grumbling that it wouldn't be that great anyways, right? A week or two escaping for vacation is great, but you'd eventually get bored with it 24/7, wouldn't you? After living in Phuket for a few years, I can wholeheartedly and exuberantly say a loud and resounding NO! Of course, my mom always wondered how anyone could ever be bored. There's always something to do!

I might have felt differently if I had lived on a smaller island that had a similar feel and lifestyle from coast to coast, with not a whole lot of variety and a constant hum of same old same old. Not Phuket.... Let me take you on a quick tour of only a few of the many personalities of Phuket:

Bang Tao Village

My first home in Phuket was nestled in a little village called Bang Tao, a local Muslim community where I was awakened by the Muezzin's call to prayer (reminiscent of my days in Dubai) and where I frequently had to wait for the chickens to cross the road or even chase them out of our garden and back into their own 'coop' next door (the polar opposite to Dubai's mega-million-dollar sky scrapers and pure 'chic'-ness). I often chuckled to myself as I remembered the old 'why did the chicken cross the road' joke and the age-old saying that someone has 'flown the coop!' There are a few resorts in town since the beach is the longest and most beautiful on the island (in my opinion) and things did get a little livelier during high season (January – March) but I could hide out in my little oasis if I wanted.

Patong Beach and Phuket Town

If I wanted to emerge from my cocoon for some 'action', the crazy tourist mecca of Patong was only a 20-minute motorbike ride away. Bangla Road is an infamous walking road with wall-to-wall bars, Muay Thai boxing rings, and cabaret shows, which you don't really need to see since the real show is swirling around you right on the street. For some historic flavour, lots of street vendors and heaps of shopping, Phuket Town is not much further away and will bring more than enough excitement to relieve any island boredom that may have set in.

Rawai Beach

If I needed a real remote, relaxing day to recover from the excitement of Patong, or just a little get away day trip, I headed to the southern most tip of the island. A short hop beyond is a pristine beach called Rawai. I often drove straight down the west coast (well, there are lots of twists and turns but you get the idea) and was rewarded at every turn by sparkling vistas of green waters, dotted with secret coves and little-known bays.

Laguna

For those who prefer to enclose themselves in an expat enclave, there are several to choose from. Laguna was the one I lived closest to that boasts miles of single-family villas, low-rise apartment buildings and its very own four and five-star resorts. It's even the host of one of the Iron Man Triathlons. If you lived there, you could really forget you're even living in an Asian country as it looks like any westernized community that could have been parachuted in from anywhere.

Side Streets and Hill Tops

Exploring down any of the many unmarked roads that have sprouted like vines from a bean-stock throughout the island will often lead to dead ends. That combined with the scarcity of road signs means most travellers will keep on going. However, ignoring the directional advice of the GPS often netted me an amazing peek at sprawling rubber tree farms as well as water falls atop mountains hidden by overgrown pathways that an adventurous spirit and trampling of weeds can easily overcome.

Never Bored

While living on Phuket, I worked as an author and freelance writer so most of my days were spent at my desk typing away. The variety of the island's 'personalities' that surrounded me provided constant inspiration to keep the creativity flowing and oodles of motivation to help me get back to work whenever a writer's block should rear its ugly square head. If a bout of island fever did sneak up and I had to get away... there was always Bangkok!

CHAPTER 4

Songkran – The Biggest Water Fight in the World

Every year, on April 13th, while living in Thailand, I would join in the Songkran celebrations. It was one of my favourite days of the year! Songkran is Thailand's New Year. It is a time for renewal, for washing away any bad luck from the past year and for hoping for health and prosperity in the year ahead.

Early in the morning as the sun rises, it is time for prayer. Buddhist worshippers head to temple to seek blessings, light candles and incense and pour scented water over the shoulder of Buddha while quietly making one special wish. This is also the time to recognise and give respect to the elders of the community.

As the day progresses, the tradition of pouring water over the shoulder of sacred statues translates into the world's biggest water fight. Locals and tourists alike arm themselves with gigantic water bazookas and ghost-buster style water backpacks. The more serious revellers hoist huge barrels of water onto the back of pick-up trucks, with each occupant prepared for battle with bucket in hand.

The temperature in Thailand in April is usually very warm, averaging 35-40 degrees Celsius, so the continual soaking is a welcome respite from the heat.

Most guidebooks say that the best Songkran celebrations are in Bangkok or Chang Mai but the parade of trucks, motorcycles and pedestrians spraying water as they go, also take over the streets of Patong, Phuket as well. It's wall-to-wall people, not only sporting various varieties of water propulsion apparatus but ear-to-ear grins as well.

"Be careful driving to Patong on your motorcycle," said Thanya who worked at the resort we were staying at in Bang Tao Beach. "People will throw buckets of water at you and want to put powder on your face for good luck, so go very slow. It's better."

Orange pylons mark most 'water stops' along the way. Several smiling faces wait to pour their pans of often ice-cold water over a willing shoulder passing by. A gentle hand placed on the side of the rider's face usually follows next, leaving behind a white chalky paste made from lye.

Those who choose not to slow down are rewarded with a bucketful of water thrown across their path anyway, aimed at the shoulder but often hitting heads and bodies broadside. It really does pay to slow down and enjoy the experience rather than getting a high velocity earful of water, which would probably end up behind an eardrum.

"It's so much fun for all ages," said one fellow reveller visiting with her family from Australia as she watched her husband and daughter in the middle of the throngs in front of the Honky Tonk Bar on Thanon Bangla Street in the heart of Patong. "The parents just become great big kids too."

With all that soap and water flying around everyone is squeaky clean by the end of the day.

For more information on Songkran visit www.tourismthailand.org.

CHAPTER 5

Phuket Vegetarian Festival

Every year, during the ninth lunar month of the Chinese calendar, the streets of Phuket ring with the sound of loud drumming as mah song are possessed by Chinese Gods and Goddesses. Rituals that cleanse and heal take place simultaneously.

The annual Phuket Vegetarian Festival runs from September 27th through October 5th. It is a celebration I enjoyed each year I lived on Phuket. The first year was an incredible experience. As I watched one of the Chinese Goddesses enter the body of Ama, a 14-year-old girl who was the daughter of a friend, she started writhing and shaking, her eyes rolling back into her head. Ama is a Shaman or medium, chosen for her purity by the Goddess to be a vessel for messages and guidance, especially during the Phuket Vegetarian Festival.

I joined the other devotees dressed in white from head to toe, and gave praise to each of the Chinese

Gods and Goddesses, handing over my burning incense in homage. Participating in the rituals brings good fortune, good health, brightness and inner peace. During the celebrations we even burned gold leaf as an offering and in return will have 'beng ang' (good luck) and be rewarded with much gold.

The festival started in 1825 after a group of opera singers fell ill while visiting Phuket from China to entertain the Chinese tin workers who had settled in Kathu District. They believed that if they ate a vegetarian diet for three days (the original detox) to honour two of the emperor gods, Kiew Ong Tai Teh and Yok Ong Sone Teh, they would be cured... and they were.

According to the Phuket Vegetarian Festival website: "It later happened that one familiar with the festival volunteered to return to Kansai, in China, where he invited the sacred Hiao Ho-le or Hiao lan (incense smoke) and Lian Tui (name plaques), which have the status of Gods, to come stay in Kathu. He also brought holy writings used in the ceremonies, returning to Phuket on the seventh night of the ninth month. The people, upon hearing of his arrival, went in procession to Bang Niao Pier to bring him and his sacred cargo back. This was the origin of the processions that figure so greatly in the festival."

Once the possession was complete, Ama, the embodiment of her Goddess, joined her compatriots who had been simultaneously taken over by other deities. They are the 'mah song' or 'horses of the Gods'. They would all carry their new hosts in a procession through town to the next Chinese temple to give praise to the all-mighty chairman, Kiew Ong Tai Teh.

I joined the procession riding in a truck in the company of a group of children who had been given the very important role of percussionists. They were responsible for keeping up the drumming and clanging of symbols throughout the two-hour long meandering through the streets of Phuket to ward off evil spirits. It was an exuberant cacophony periodically amplified by others we passed on the roadside who also offered food and drink to the Gods.

It is always a joyful day punctuated by dramatic, even shocking demonstrations including self-cutting of the back and lips by some of the mah song with sharp axes (I've seen the blood with my own eyes) and puncturing of the cheeks with spikes and swords. They claim that while they are possessed, they feel no pain. It was so unbelievable as I watched one young man slice his bottom lip open that I couldn't bring myself to pull my camera out. But the image will remain in my mind's eye for a very long time. He didn't even flinch. Such is the strength and passion of his commitment and belief in his religion.

To learn more visit www.phuketvegetarian.com.

Anne Louise O'Connell

CHAPTER 6

Exploring the Outskirts

When living the expat lifestyle or even just traveling long-term, it is important to establish a routine. Each time you move to a new country, routine is what will help you ease into life in a new place. However, try not to get too lulled by the boring rhythm of the coffee mornings, school pick-up (if you have kids), stop 'n shop, mani-pedi type routine. You've got to shake it up once in a while.

After living in Thailand for a couple of years, I got into a nice routine. I started a writers' group that met once a month and I helped out regularly with a local charity. Then I worked on whatever writing project I had underway the rest of the time. Sometimes I had to remind myself that I lived in a different (quite exotic) country and to make a point of exploring beyond the local grocery store once in a while. When living as an expat, it is highly advisable to ensure you have the most enriching experience possible.

I have a friend (also an expat) who came to visit a couple of times and spurred this philosophy on. During one visit we did a side trip to Phi Phi Island. The next time, before she came, she asked "What remote island shall we visit this time?" I had to put my thinking cap on.

We were blessed with being surrounded by natural beauty in our immediate vicinity but also with a veritable feast of options for places to explore, including hundreds of islands in Chalong and Phang Nga Bays. This time I chose the very remote, not touristy, peaceful island of Koh Yao Yai.

There are a few words of advice I'd like to share when planning to explore those 'outskirts' wherever you live or when travelling unknown territory:

- First, suspend any and all expectation that the usual meticulously organized itinerary that you might normally plan is actually going to unfold as you imagine.

- Second, be open to change and embrace it with a smile and an adventurous spirit!

Here's what unfolded for us . . . our plan was to take a taxi to Bang Rong pier and catch a long tail boat at noon for 50 baht (which is what I had read on the internet was the cost) and enjoy the leisurely one-hour ride across to the island. I had laid out a budget for the excursion as I had also read that there are no ATM machines on the island and anything off the resort would be 'cash only'. No worries . . . or as they say in Thailand, 'mai bpen rai'!

Upon arrival at the pier, I asked for two tickets to Koh Yao Yai (there is a smaller sister island called Koh Yao Noi so you don't want to wind up on the wrong island). I was told speedboat ferry tickets were 200 baht each. *Silly man*, I thought, we wanted adventure . . . so I asked how much for the long tail boat. He answered, "150 baht." Hmmm . . . I explained that I had seen on the Internet that it was 50 baht and the fellow selling the tickets smiled and said, "Maybe 10 years ago."

The outcome of this exchange? Well, we opted for the speedboat, which left an hour earlier than the long tail boat and took half an hour instead of an hour and was only 50 baht (or about $2.00 Canadian) more. We'd leave the long tail adventure for another time. We realized our decision was the right one as we came out through the cut into the open water and a high wind had kicked up the sea to a two-to-three-foot chop! We would have been pretty uncomfortable (not to mention drenched when we got there) had we taken the smaller, slower conveyance.

Upon arrival at Klong Hai Pier we were picked up by the resort (Koh Yao Yai Village Resort part of the Treasury Village Group) in a typical local bus, which is a pick up truck with open-air awning over the back with bench seats down both sides. Love it! We enjoyed the view during the 20-minute, slightly dusty ride and were greeted with cooling, wet, lemon-scented towels as we pulled up. The welcome and check-in was 5-Star (it's rated a 4 on Trip Advisor but I'd give it full stars!) and the resort was peaceful and serene. Our villa was like a tree house, perched on stilts, surrounded by jungle. We thoroughly enjoyed the royal treatment, amazing views, delicious menu, wrap around infinity pool and a spectacular full moon after dinner.

We topped our adventure off with a tour of the southern part of the island on motor bikes.

This exploration on the 'outskirts' of my home on Phuket was definitely a successful mission.

CHAPTER 7

Fun Phuket Tourist Traps

I've always loved being a tourist in my own town. I'll never tire of visiting Citadel Hill in Halifax, Nova Scotia, where I grew up and spent the first 26 years of my life. It's a step back in the past, where you can get lost amongst the ramparts of the old fort and walk amidst period-costumed people and really get a feel of what it was like in the 'olden days'. I have probably had this 'one-of-a-kind' experience about a hundred times. Then there was the Jungle Queen in Fort Lauderdale, an old-style paddleboat that took a lazy cruise down the Intracoastal Waterway to a real-life Seminole Indian camp with alligator wrestling! In Dubai, it was camel rides in the desert and a hair-raising elevator ride to the 124th floor of the tallest building in the world to the observation deck of the Burj Khalifa.

It was no different in Thailand where I easily fell into my old MO (modus operandi) of acting like a tourist wherever I hang my hat. I think it makes for a more enjoyable life. I visited Thailand several times before we moved there so have happily swum with the elephants in Koh Chang, and visited the famous Doi Suthep temple in Chang Mai.

Having lived in Phuket for four years, I'd like to share my top five 'tourist traps' that you can't help but get caught in... more than once!

1 – Songkran

I experienced Songkran every year that I lived in Thailand. This is Thai New Year, which is celebrated in April. It's known as the biggest water fight in the world and everyone is armed to the teeth with super soakers, buckets of water, back pack blasters and a pasty soap concoction to smear on your face for good measure. Like Christmas, there is a religious origin to it, but the fun of soaking your neighbour and even complete strangers, does slightly overshadow the real meaning of Songkran, which is a time to pay your respect to your elders and to Buddha (by washing the elders' hands in rose water and the shoulder of a statue of Buddha in the temple, hence the water's role in the celebrations). It is also a time for renewal as it's the beginning of spring.

2 – The Cabaret Show at Nok & Joe's

This one is a well-hidden trap unless you find yourself in Bang Tao Village. Then you can't miss this block-long, driftwood adorned, Canadian flag flying eatery. Nok & Joe's is a wonderful bar/restaurant with a lot of character, mostly because of Joe who is from Calgary, Alberta (Canada) who built the building as well as all the gnarly bar stools and other whimsical furniture. He greets his customers wearing his cowboy hat, cowboy boots and wrangler jeans no matter how hot it gets! Every Sunday night (Wednesday too during high season) there's a huge buffet BBQ and a cabaret show featuring some of the top ladyboy performers from Patong (#3 on the list). Of course, Nok's culinary skill is greatly appreciated too. It's true authentic Thai food. After all, she is a local.

3 - Patong (the whole darn town)

This trap has big teeth and is not for the feint of heart. I have to really be in the mood for crowds and partying to head to Patong but it is a must see and I did see it many times while living close by (about a 30-minute ride on the motorbike). On a busy night, the main street, Soi Bangla, is wall-to-wall people.

The street is closed to traffic so picture a street party, a la Mardi Gras, every single night with loud music, dancing in the streets and more than a little inebriated behaviour. So, gird your loins before you go and keep your hands to yourself . . . the wild life may bite.

4 - The Big Buddha

On the more serene side of the coin, a visit to the Phuket Big Buddha is breath taking because of both the sheer size of it and the spectacular panoramic view of the island that you can behold (Chalong Bay on one side and the Andaman Sea on the other). The building of the Buddha was funded totally by donations (there is a marble tile with my name on it built into the base – I couldn't help but make a contribution). The imposing statue is 45 metres high and 25 metres across at the base. Inside, you can visit and pray with the monks who make their home in the temple underneath the statue.

5 - Phuket Fantasy

Admittedly, I only experienced this particular tourist trap once but I did see the buses go by every day loaded with eager spectators. According to the website it's "The ultimate cultural theme park" and I would concur. My favourite part was the ginormous buffet but the main attraction is an elephant show, traditional Thai dancing and music and theatrical performances. There are several restaurants, fire works and street performers too.

There's a whole lot more to explore on the little island paradise of Phuket for those with an open mind and an adventurous spirit.

CHAPTER 8

Motorbike Mash-up

We've probably all heard the often-glorious results when two different songs of totally unrelated genres are combined in a 'mash-up' of vocal styling and creative manipulations of music scores. It's not so pretty when the 'mash-up' is a combo of expats, tourists and locals buzzing around a busy island on motorbikes, vying for the coveted spots in the narrow tunnel between lanes of cars.

Yes, I have to admit, while living in Thailand I did succumb to the heady lure of not having to sit in gridlocked traffic in the busier parts of the island, like Phuket Town, Patong and the dreaded traffic circle at Heroine's Monument. I drove a motorbike and I did find myself giggling away as I blasted by motorists, fuming in their cars as the third or fourth light changes to red and they still haven't moved more than a few feet. It was exhilarating!

However, as I was carefully manoeuvring the

twists and turns on the road from Bang Tao to Kamala one day I found myself shaking my head at every turn and praying for 'high season' to end. It's no wonder that there is a spike in motorbike accidents during that time of year because the rules of the road and just basic common sense are broken more often than they're followed.

So, after a few years of 'riding the hog' (okay, it's more like a scooter but allow me to dream), here are a few dos and don'ts for both newbies and experienced riders, because we can all use a reminder:

Do's

- Do wear a helmet. I know it's not as cool as letting the wind whip through your hair and the resulting 'helmet-head' is less than attractive but statistics don't lie . . . helmets do save lives. And, you can get some pretty cool ones with any type of design your heart desires. I actually had several and chose according to what matched my ensemble of the day. And, do grab a colourful 'do-rag' to top if off!

- Do develop eyes on the back of your head or at least pay attention to everything around you, including what's coming up from behind. I learned to adjust my mirrors every time I got on the bike because even if I had them in the perfect configuration the last time I rode it, someone had inevitably bumped into them or parked two inches away and leaned on them and knocked them out of kilter.

- Do wear shoes. Actually, long sleeves and long pants are highly recommended but, come on! It's an island that sometimes hits temperatures of 44 Celsius, so I admit I certainly didn't but I have seen some nasty road burn that could have been avoided if a little more skin had been covered up. Wearing shoes is a no-brainer, as you never know when you have to plant your feet in a hurry and what sharp objects could be lurking below, not to mention the hot asphalt!

Don'ts

- Don't drive on the gravel shoulder to pass a car unless you can see way ahead that there aren't any obstacles, such as the humongous pothole I careened into one day and almost got catapulted into the ditch. Fortunately, I kept my wits about me, my hands on the handlebars and braked appropriately and thank God there was no one stupidly following close behind. It would have been ugly!

- Don't pile the whole family on one bike. I know it's the conveyance of choice for Thai families of four or five, but they've been doing it since birth so are more comfortable and competent with multiple riders.

- Don't drive two or three abreast and have a conversation with your buds while going 60 km/hour while traffic builds up behind you. So uncool.

If you're a new arrival and you've never driven on the left-hand side of the road (like myself as I grew up in Canada, and the two other countries I lived in before Thailand also drove on the 'right' side) get comfortable with the concept before driving either a motorbike or a car. I'm not sure if my brain is wired differently but I did find it more natural to drive on the left. Back in Canada I have to consciously remind myself from one minute to the next to stay to the right.

It's amazing what you can get used to when you have to. One of my favourite sayings is 'necessity is the mother of invention,' which is often attributed to the philosopher, Plato. I wonder what Plato would say if he saw Thailand's motorcycle mash-up? Perhaps one of his famous sayings like: "Good actions give strength to ourselves and inspire good actions in others." Wherever you travel in the world, drive carefully!

CHAPTER 9

Wandering Around any 'Old Town'

When getting to know a new place, whether just visiting, or moving there for good, learning about the history and culture is always in the top three of the 'must do' list for me. If it's a place steeped in centuries of history it's always a treat to explore the 'old town' if there is such a thing, and visit any preserved historical sites, taking in the architecture, ambiance and aromas.

Phuket doesn't disappoint. An afternoon excursion into Phuket's 'Old Town' at the heart of the main city, rewards visitors with the colourful glory of Sino-Colonial architecture. Mansions built by tin Baron's in the 18th century still stand and streets are peppered with ancient herb shops, fabric sellers and tailors. Wandering in and out of hand carved, Thai-style furniture shops and visiting both Chinese and Buddhist temples creates a rich, cultural experience that leaves quite an impression. After my first visit, when we returned home my clothes still had the pungent aroma of a collection of herbs and spices from our visit to the 'Oldest Herbs Shop' in Phuket. A popular stop on the walking tour is to have tea at the historic China Inn, which doubles as an antique and craft shop.

The strongest cultural influences on the island and its history were Chinese and British. However, several others have left their mark as well like the Burmese, French, Japanese and Indians. The infusion of certain elements of each of these country's cultures has created the multi-dimensional, multi-coloured fabric of the Thai culture we enjoy today.

During our tour, we meandered past the Phuket Thai Hua Museum, which was built in 1911 originally as a Chinese school but, unfortunately, we didn't have time to go in. I'll save that for another day along with the Old Phuket Town post office, built in 1932, which is now the home of the Phuket Philatelic Museum. I might skip that one since I'm not a stamp collector!

Every year there is a three-day celebration called the Phuket Old Town Cultural Festival. The purpose of the festival is to preserve Thailand's culture and traditions and to put the spotlight on cultural tourism. Festivities kick off with a parade through the streets of Old Town with dancers and musicians and traditional Chinese dragons.

The history of Phuket, as far back as 500 BC, has been recorded in a lengthy tome (more like a textbook) written by a Scottish expat named Colin Mackay. In *The History of Phuket and the Surrounding Region*, published in 2013, he tracks the evolution of Phuket from the Bronze Age through to the tin mining boom that started in the mid 1940s and waned in the 70s as the tourism industry began to grow. I met Mackay when I attended the launch of his book, hosted by the American Chamber of Commerce at the Royal Phuket Marina. He notes in the preface that the majority of the history is told from the perspective of foreigners, and says, "This is mainly because comparatively few old Thai historical records were kept and even fewer have survived. Therefore, it was the European, Chinese, Indian and Middle Eastern visitors over the centuries who have left the most, and in many periods, the only, historical records about Phuket and the central peninsula region." However, he does give credit (and lots of praise) to Thai historian, Pranee Sakulpipatana for helping him dig up records, stay on track and ensure the Thai perspective was well represented.

So, Phuket has been an expat enclave for centuries, paving the way for the likes of us and leaving a lasting legacy for our enjoyment.

CHAPTER 10

You Can EAT That?

While living in Bang Tao, I would go walking in the morning with my Thai friend, Kanrutai (fondly known as Kan). I had complained that I didn't have time for exercise because I had so many writing projects on the go. She took me at my word and solved the problem for me by calling at 6:30 one sunny morning and asking sweetly if I was ready to go.

I do love to walk. I love to inhale all the sights, sounds and smells of nature and watch the birds and butterflies flit across my path and over my head; listen to the wind in the trees and the crash of the waves on the beach. Walking with Kan opened my eyes to a whole new world and brought a new appreciation of my surroundings. There's nothing like seeing a place that you've seen many times but through the eyes of someone else (especially a local).

I've done lots of educational hikes in evergreen

forests, thick steamy jungles, rolling hills and rocky mountains all over the globe but strolling with Kan takes the cake . . . literally. The first walk we went on together she took me down unexplored laneways and around unfamiliar corners. I loved every minute, listening to her stories of growing up on a rubber tree farm in northern Thailand. At one point, she stopped abruptly and pointed to a deep purple flower and said, "This very good in salad or can make good drink." Huh? It looked like a pansy to me.

She proceeded to describe how to boil the flower and then drain the liquid, put it in the fridge and once it's cooled down, pour it over ice and it's delicious! I'm not a cook so usually when someone starts to tell me about any type of recipe my eyes glaze over and I start thinking about the next chapter of my novel or I start doing a mental outline of a client's book while I wait for the droning to stop. But, when Kan started describing what to do with these little purple flowers that hung like wallpaper along the side of the road, I was riveted. According to Kan, "It's also good for when you hurt to make pee-pee." So, then I knew what to do when I couldn't find any cranberry juice in the Tesco Lotus (the local grocery store).

The next day's meandering didn't disappoint. It netted us a bushel of lovely green vines that to me looked like the spouts that sprung off of the beanstalk that Jack climbed in one of my all-time favourite childhood stories. Kan meticulously untwined one strand at a time from a smattering of bushes and twigs, running up and down the main drag between Bang Tao Village and Surin Beach. She claimed that after a little steaming to take the bitterness out, it would make a perfect side dish. She was like a kid in a candy store, skipping along the sidewalk shrieking with laughter with every new find.

Kan didn't know the English words for our culinary roadside delights so I went online in search of information to reassure me that I wasn't being told a tall tale! I thought maybe her giggles meant that she was trying to tease me. I found a plethora of sites touting the huge variety of edible plants (both nutritional and medicinal) that can be found throughout Thailand. So, she really wasn't pulling my leg. The best I can figure is that the vine Kan was giddily gathering was called Pak Tam Leung and, just like spinach, can be lightly steamed and eaten as a tasty and healthy side dish.

Don't even get me started on the herbs that grow wild in Thailand. I may not be much of a cook but I do love to eat. Part of our meandering typically included crushing a few leaves between our fingers and inhaling the pungent smell of a wild basil or coriander leaf. Yum!

The downside to this treasure trove of delectable treats is that there's often poisonous stuff intertwined with the good stuff and to the untrained eye it all looks exactly the same. My love of hiking in the woods started in the wilds of Canada where I always counted on other more educated guides to watch out for any poison ivy. I've never been able to tell if I'm walking in it or not. So, the moral of this story is, if you're planning to do a little shopping in the woods, you had better take someone knowledgeable with you.

CHAPTER 11

The Thailand De-tox

During an out of the ordinary getaway, the phrase 'early to bed early to rise' took on a whole new meaning for me. Each morning at 7 a.m. there was a knock on my bungalow door, which I opened to a broadly grinning Tong, whose bright and cheery greeting was always "Good morning! Watermelon or pineapple today?" It was the perfect way to start each morning of the eight-day fasting de-tox I had committed to on the beautiful island of Koh Samui in Thailand.

The Thailand de-tox has become very popular among expats and travellers alike, who often come from other parts of Thailand and Southeast Asia and sometimes from even greater distances for 'the cleanse'.

"Many of our guests, who are predominantly foreigners, come back every year, especially if they have an inner awareness of what their body needs," co-founder of Health Oasis Resort, Mel Loverh told me. "They search for it; they value it and they will travel long distances for it. They're the ones who value it the most of anyone because expats and travellers tend to have a higher level of stress."

During my week, I met several Brits, some of whom were expats, some were not; a fellow Canadian who listened to my expat stories dreaming of the day she would break away; an American screenwriter from Florida; and a few folks from Australia - one expat who had been living abroad for a year who was a yoga teacher studying naturopathy after a long and stressful career in advertising.

I initially began my de-tox research for a feature article with the intention of interviewing Debbie Nicol, an Australian expat living in Dubai who had just completed her fourth 'cleansing' at Health Oasis. I also interviewed the owners, Loverh and Dr. Manta Darnswat and was so intrigued by the process that I decided to do the program myself and experience it first-hand.

Many people 'do the de-tox' for weight loss but according to Loverh, "It's really more of a tool towards raising your vibration and self-awareness than for weight loss or anything else. The weight loss is an added benefit."

I still did ask Nicol about her passion for the

'de-tox' in order to delve a little more deeply into one's motivation for many return visits.

"I have now gone to de-tox at Health Oasis, a small and very basic 'village-type' setting right on the beach, four times," said Nicol. "Some people de-tox yearly for three days, others do it more often and for longer. For me, I allow my body to tell me when it needs it," she said. "My first one had a purpose to 'unstick or unblock' me – I had no idea or expectation for the additional benefit of weight loss," Nicol continues. "However, when I had such great results, I promised myself to change my lifestyle and to watch what I eat more, as it really is about changing your habits. I knew I'd be back if I could keep that weight off. I did two trips in six months, then the third was 18 months later, and then one for the ten-day 'Total Transformation' program about 26 months after."

Co-founder, Dr. Manta, is a doctor of Chinese medicine specializing in naturopathy and her partner and husband, Loverh is an herbalist specializing in western, Chinese and South American herbs. Health Oasis is licensed by the Thailand Department of Health as a Traditional Medicine Hospital, which was very reassuring for me.

I chose the 'Nurture' program and the schedule was chock a block with daily yoga and massage, which I took full advantage of, along with the less pleasant ingesting of a psyllium/bentonite mixture that promised to grab onto all the nasty toxins in my digestive tract, colon and bowel and help move it forward to elimination! The psyllium shake alternated every hour and a half with a battery of minerals, herbs and antioxidants. Each day was punctuated with either one or two colonics. This was my least favourite part but the thought of how thoroughly it was 'cleansing' my insides made it tolerable. I was also promised that at the end of the eight days, I would be given a flora implant that would enter my colon and replace the good bacteria, which would have been flushed out right along with the bad.

Dr. Manta is like a den mother watching over her brood, bringing out various potions and concoctions to ease particular physical (and sometimes emotional) reactions (both can be triggered by the release of toxins as your body relieves itself of the burden). Or, to just lend a listening ear and give advice on healthy eating or share insight into the realm of holistic healing.

I loved that everything was taken with lots of freshly made fruit and vegetable juices, unlimited water (actually three litres a day was recommended), herbal tea and vegetable broth.

My bungalow was right on the beach and kayaks sat at the ready any time I wanted. I swam in the oxygenated pool, and availed myself of a nightly herbal steam. I got used to seeing the goats grazing under my balcony and watching the old man walking his miniature pony down the beach just after sunrise. It was idyllic.

"Every year I escape to a magical place for one or two weeks," said Sofie Skjold Halkjær from Denmark who had been at Health Oasis the same week as Nicol. "I do it because I have no choice, my body screams for it. I've learned to listen to my body, which is very sensitive. At first, I was stressed about how many things I had to do during the day but after I calmed down, I really enjoyed it and will come back."

Halkjær is a mother and stepmother, trying to juggle the needs of a combined family, and a new business as well as her own personal needs. She believes her time away and the de-tox process is both a physical and emotional release and, when complete, allows her to return to her family refreshed. "I am able to re-connect to the kids and create a flow in the family again".

Halkjær talked about her initial stress levels along with an upset stomach and fever blisters. I had no adverse reactions other than a little lightheadedness on day two from low blood sugar, which was alleviated easily by drinking more juice. What I did release was eight pounds! However, above all else, I felt better than I had in years.

It's always important to consider possible side effects. Detox diets that severely limit protein or that require fasting, for example, can result in fatigue. Long-term fasting can result in vitamin and mineral deficiencies. Colon cleansing, which is often recommended as part of a detox plan, can cause cramping, bloating, nausea and vomiting. Dehydration also can be a concern.

I didn't have any of these symptoms, however, my friend, an Aussie living in Thailand, had most of them but still came out on the other side feeling great.

"Cleansing reactions indicate a healing crisis at work and do not last, unless we stubbornly resist," says Loverh. "Healing crises are part of the body's natural detoxification mechanism, bringing each layer of toxins to the surface and flushing them out as the original cause of the problem is rebalanced."

I just knew that I had 'toxic overload'. As I learned about the process, and heard more anecdotal feedback from people who had done the de-tox, no amount of western medicine's scepticism could dissuade me. I believed that my body needed a little assistance.

The benefits vary from person to person. Nicol shared that in her experience she has seen multiple benefits.

"Everyone has different reactions according to

our differing needs," said Nicol. "The benefit of my first detox was the shock factor to actually see what I had done to my body over the years . . . and that becomes evident with the colonics. That spurred me on to respect that which I've been given by nature, and to understand its mechanics, and to realize it's only as good as the care I give it."

Nicol went on to explain that the second benefit was the feeling of peace that you get. However, her 'peace' came in disguise.

"I always have good days and bad days, like the day my energy was so low I could barely walk from my room— surrendering to that was actually a form of peace," she said. "I am usually rewarded the next day with huge amounts of energy. I've seen many different reactions to de-tox from high energy, to crying, to breaking out in blemishes, to sweating. Having said that, the uniqueness of Health Oasis is the closeness you forge with others and the support we give each other. It may be as small as a comment like 'it will pass' or a chat about how it affected you. You learn a lot about each other in short time, yet if you prefer to stick to yourself, that's okay too."

The biggest concerns that seemed to permeate all the negative articles on the benefits (or lack thereof) of de-tox programs revolve around not getting enough nutrients, not monitoring for any adverse reactions, eliminating the 'good' bacteria long with the bad, and the possibility of perforating the bowel during colonics.

These are all worth exploring and each issue was addressed in the orientation upon arrival when the process is thoroughly explained and any questions or concerns are answered.

In developing the program Loverh and Dr. Manta recognized the potential downside of fasting so introduced a battery of herbs and supplements to counter the loss of nutrients. Spirulina, which is organically grown and provides over 100 vital nutrients (amino acids, vitamins, enzymes and essential fatty acids), is taken twice a day as well as a liquefied mixture of 22 herbs taken five times a day. The mixture includes herbs such as dandelion (good for the kidney), juniper, parsley, myrrh, cayenne, ginger, St Mary's Thistle, rhubarb, rosehips, hawthorn, Siberian ginseng, turmeric, and angelica to name a few.

"These are applied and held under the tongue to ensure proper absorption into the body. It's more potent and direct with no side effects," said Loverh. "Taking tablets is less efficient because when you're fasting your digestive juices take a break so the tablets don't get broken down. Most of the good is lost in 'elimination'. The shake is mixed with juice to sustain your blood sugar level so your body doesn't go into crisis mode."

The little pink basket that was assigned to me on day one also included guarana for extra energy, chlorophyll to accelerate blood cleansing, colloidal silver to boost the immune system and ocean trace minerals.

I felt confident that the all-natural process that had been developed by Loverh and Dr. Manta, over the past 20 years of documented experimentation, with a scientific approach to fine-tuning 'the cleanse' could only be good for me and cause me no harm. And, I was thankful that the basket came with a very detailed schedule of what to take and when, with plenty of staff on hand to clear up any confusion.

According to Loverh, fasting is a form of healing that affects every part of you from the physical, to the emotional and mental and even spiritual. It provides a feeling of clarity; working on an emotional level and makes your organs work in a more efficient way.

Loverh and Dr. Manta founded Health Oasis in 1997 as a healing centre, health community and alternative school that welcomed any practitioner who wanted to live on the grounds and contribute whatever healing modality was their specialty.

"You were meant to fulfil yourself and be inspired to live a balanced life with everyone contributing their expertise," recollected Loverh. "I had no idea it was going to get so popular. It was my personal practice, nothing else, and I studied the different healing modalities for my own benefit."

Sixteen years later, it has evolved into a cleansing and de-tox holiday escape mostly for expats living in Asia but also attracting tourists from the UK, Australia and even as far away as the United States. When the resort first opened the guests were predominantly female (90/10) and now the mix is about 50/50.

Programs are three, five, eight, and ten days or longer. "The repair you've done in 10 days will change your life," claims Loverh. "The change is deep, dramatic and irreversible. Once you've taken this step, you can't undo the good that's been done."

Loverh shares that the secret to staying healthy after 'the cleanse' is not to be too strict and deny yourself. If you do and then you cheat, you feel terrible guilt. He advises guests to empower themselves to let go occasionally, take responsibility for their choices without being ignorant. "The inner conflict is a worse energy than the bad food or habit could ever be," he says.

"The measure for me is when I get back on the airplane headed home and look at the bread roll and think – I don't need that – that tells me I'm feeling a lot more respect for my body," says Nicol.

The selection of spas and de-tox facilities throughout Thailand are absolutely endless, from the five-star luxury of Absolute Sanctuary to the rustic, family operated Health Oasis, both located on Koh Samui. There are also many options in Phuket, Chang Mai and even Bangkok, if you prefer the big city atmosphere.

When my eight days were up, I really could have done more. I felt refreshed and clear-headed. Armed with my 'after fast eating plan' I headed home to Phuket with a whole new attitude towards living healthy in my expat world. I will not scold myself if I give in to temptation but will regularly include a fruit fasting day to re-set the clock and also look forward to my next fasting de-tox.

This article was originally published in Global Living *magazine.*

CHAPTER 12

Thailand Island Hopping in Style

A slow, meandering island hopping over several days on a chartered sailboat is a great get away if you have loads of time. Exploring groups of islands has been a popular pastime for me over the years. I've done most of the Caribbean and many of the Greek Isles but seeing several islands in one day is a unique opportunity that can be elusive. Enter Thailand's Phang Nga Bay and the surrounding area.

In the book *1001 Places to See Before You Die*, Phang Nga Bay is high on the list for visitors and residents of Southeast Asia. Described by the author as "an obstacle course of limestone monoliths," the natural rock formations are awe-inspiring and draw self-proclaimed explorers in a variety of conveyances.

I discovered that the best way to explore several of these remote and pristine beauties is by procuring the services of a private speedboat, complete with local captain and guide.

It's a great option for people who want to go at their own pace and don't want to share with loads of tourists. You can book a tour but it's the typical cattle call experience... huge tour boats absorbing hundreds of tourists with color-coded dots slapped on their chests who shuffle up the gangway and squeeze into spaces on hard wooden benches not wide enough for a four-year-old (who inevitably has to sit on someone's lap as the last lines are tossed from the dock and the overflowing tour boat pulls away).

Those in the know steer away from these, choosing to investigate a little further afield with a more exclusive, tailor-made plan.

The private tours range from elegant, champagne-drinking, sunset tours to more adventurous options for who are willing to rough it a bit. The guides will avoid the crowds as much as possible, which is not always easy and takes some manoeuvring by the captains to get into some of the more out of the way places, but it's a more peaceful and enjoyable experience.

Whether it's a tour boat or private speed boat, the agenda could possibly include one of two islands in the area that Hollywood has made famous: Koh Phing Kan (otherwise known as James Bond Island) and Koh Phi Phi Leh, **the** beach that Leonardo

DiCaprio swam 1.5 kilometres to reach (in the movie anyway).

A quick stop at these overly popular spots is okay but I prefer to spend the majority of my time enjoying the spectacular vistas of sheer moss-colour cliffs that spring up like the mythical Kraken; and exploring the wonders of caves dug out over the centuries by persistent sea water, where archaeological digs have uncovered signs of prehistoric life and are said to house spirits from the past. These caves are also a favourite nesting place for small birds called swiftlets and the scene of the controversial harvesting of nests for bird's nest soup, which is a delicacy in the Asian culture.

Coral Seekers' skippers, like Captain Keng who has been with them for 16 years, filled with generations of local insights and knowledge of the best, unspoiled coves and anchorages, create an experience not soon forgotten.

He shared stories of sea gypsy lore while we cruised along, searching for the perfect spot where we could immerse ourselves in the emerald-green, reinvigorating sea and snorkel amongst the rainbow bursts of green and red parrot fish, yellow and black striped sergeant majors, orange and white clown fish and spectacular, spikey lion fish.

For a more rigorous exploration there are always the long-tail boats, or even the quieter sea kayak option. Going solo, you can slip in and around the narrowest passageways and into the ubiquitous *hongs* (hidden rooms inside rock formations), through tunnels and caverns and under the intricate overhangs, sometimes ducking to avoid stalactites that seem eerily animated. If that does appeal, the James Bond Island full day itinerary with Coral Seekers has an optional one-hour sea kayak tour that can be added.

We topped off the adventure with sunset cocktails at Chokdee Restaurant on tiny Kai Nui Island (only accessible by small boat). The rustic ambiance was speckled with an odd assortment of characters that looked like they'd been kissed by the tropical sun and slightly spackled by the Andaman Sea, and may even have swum in from a yacht anchored beyond the protective reef. The entire island can be booked for private parties for 15 or more guests.

All Coral Seekers' captains hail from the local area, having grown up in the sea gypsy village of Rawai. Their ancestors are the original inhabitants of Phuket who lived off the sea.

The guides are also Thai and are certified by the Tourism Authority of Thailand to lead tours for the entire region – Phuket, Phang Nga and Krabi and all the sea in between.

We also visited one of the floating sea gypsy villages to experience a whole different way of life.

The floating island of Koh Panyee is popular, complete with a colourful market for shopping and local restaurants from which the pungent smell of a curry simmering wafts throughout the walkways. There was a real community feel as we were serenaded by the lilting call to prayer emanating from the Mosque's speakers and the sound of children's laughter ringing from the FIFA regulation football field.

A lot of the bay can be covered in one day but it's impossible to see all 401 square kilometres so there are suggested island groupings to make the best of a full or half day's adventure. Coral Seekers' options include a twilight snorkelling tour with romantic beach dinner for two or a romantic get away with wine and flowers.

Expats who have made Southern Thailand their home often take advantage of the popular day trips. The protected bay is pleasant most of the year but it's advisable to avoid monsoon season in July and August. The bay has multiple personalities no matter what season it is and the captains will know which days are better for which itineraries based on the relative calmness of the sea and the direction of the wind and currents.

Like most private speedboat rental companies, Coral Seekers caters to special occasions as well as corporate events with tailored programs (and menus) to meet individual needs. One company even combined their corporate retreat with volunteering for a local charity that Coral Seekers supports.

I heard a story of one group that was planning an event and asked for a Bengal tiger! Then there was the bride who arrived to her beach wedding on an elephant and a monkey participating as a ring bearer. I guess no request is too crazy here!

Originally published in Global Living *magazine, December 2012.*

CHAPTER 13

Jakarta, Indonesia

As we were planning our move to the other side of the world, we promised we would take advantage of our geographic locale and see parts of the world we wouldn't have otherwise even contemplated.

After moving to Dubai in the UAE, my first foray outside of the country was to Jakarta, Indonesia. I had been to Indonesia before but it was the more popular tourist destination of Bali. This was a place of which I had only a vague notion.

A recommendation from someone who knew Jakarta well recommended exploring beyond the beaten track (which I love to do anyways) and visit a village called Bandung about 2 ½ hours outside of Jakarta.

It was a rainy day and it had been raining on and off for many weeks. We hired a car for the day that picked us up at the hotel.

"You like music?" the driver asked as we got into the car. He had a radio station on that was playing local music so it was a great way to get in the mood to explore.

"Sure, just not too loud so we can talk," I suggested. When travelling I always ask a lot of questions whenever there's an opportunity to interact with someone 'in the know'.

The driver was happy to oblige and regaled us with stories about each town we drove through. Where there were trees and grass, everything was lush and green but in between there were clusters of dilapidated shacks, one on top of the other, with clotheslines strung between corrugated tin roofs hung with garments of all shapes and sizes, from infant one-sies to adult coveralls. It seemed sad to me but there were children playing in the yards and mothers sweeping the front porches (such as they were). Our driver laughed a lot and had a big smile on his face the whole time. Even amidst grinding poverty the people seemed so happy. I tried to ask questions about what it was like to live in Jakarta but most of the time it was hard to understand what he was saying. So, I just listened intently for the nuggets that I could understand, enjoyed the ride and his pleasant companionship.

As we approached Bandung the communities became a little more upscale and as we entered the busy streets of downtown, which was a bustle of activity, it was clear that free enterprise was alive and well.

The traffic was bumper to bumper and, like most busy Asian cities, hundreds of scooters whipped in and around the cars and congregated at the front of the line waiting for the light to turn green. It's a spectacle that never ceases to amaze me, specifically, the fact that there aren't more accidents. However, most drivers yield to the buzzing, motorized, two-wheelers and everyone goes on with their business.

The main drag was wall-to-wall outlet stores culminating in a huge mall at the centre of town. Not being big shoppers, we wandered up and down the street in search of a restaurant that was open (forgetting it was Ramadan and we were in a predominantly Muslim country). It didn't dawn on us until we were on our way back and the sun was setting and our driver finally reached for the bottle of water that had remained untouched all day long.

"Have you been fasting today?" I asked. He nodded happily (his natural state of being). I felt like a jerk since we had asked him to join us for lunch, which he had politely declined, of course.

We had eventually found a restaurant where we had lunch on a lovely patio overlooking the tree-lined street. The rain had finally let up so it was very pleasant. In Bandung there was no law banning eating and drinking in public during Ramadan, as it was in Dubai. The lack of open restaurants was due to the fact that most of them were Muslim-owned and were simply closed until sunset.

CHAPTER 14

Exploring Malaysia – Sights, Sounds & Smells

In the year or two leading to retirement, we started getting serious about where we would like to live in those 'golden years'. During 14 years of living in Florida we had done a fair bit of sailing in the Caribbean so a long-time dream was to retire on a sailboat and just bob around re-visiting islands we had been to and exploring ones we hadn't. Then a move to Dubai opened our eyes to a whole new part of the world and we turned our attention to Asia. Our first vacation after moving to Dubai was Thailand . . . we were hooked! But, not wanting to make a final decision before checking out a few other places, we headed to Malaysia, thinking that Kuala Lumpur or Penang might be a good option. Our visit there convinced us that Thailand suited us better but it didn't stop us from having a little adventure.

The Mountains of Penang, Malaysia

After a harrowing hour circling the downtown of Kuala Lumpur (KL) trying to find our way out after picking up our rental car, it was time to head to quieter environs. We knew that 'big city living' wasn't likely to be on our top three choices of retirement locales and the few days we spent in KL were enough to convince us that we were right. As much as I loved seeing the Petronas Towers and picturing Sean Connery and Catherine Zeta Jones racing after each other between buildings, it wasn't enough to entice me to live there 24/7. We liked the idea of island living better so off we went to explore Penang.

My favourite holiday moments are those that are unanticipated and unexpected like the Taoist Temple we happened upon in the mountains of Penang.

A very small, non-descript sign with an arrow pointing up a narrow, winding pathway beckoned us, even though we didn't know what the sign said. As we picked our way carefully up the steep hill a structure started to appear through the trees and we could hear the soft chanting of a group of monks.

A volunteer who quietly introduced herself as Sally offered us a cup of Chrysanthemum tea with honey and brown sugar. She was surprised when we said we had found the temple on our own and not with a tour.

She told us that the chief priest had passed away and it was the 100th day of mourning—the celebration of the spirit.

It was a peaceful place hidden in the lush rain forest. As usual in our meandering ways, turning wherever a new road took us, we found this treasure purely by accident. I love being an 'accidental tourist'. It's when the most interesting adventures happen and you meet the best people.

More colourful characters presented themselves to me when we returned to KL. As I sat beside a woman on the light rail transit (LRT), she struck up a conversation with me. It just so happened that her brother was a doctor in my hometown of Halifax, NS (Dr. Kenny Yee). She had a big, friendly smile on her face. Her kids lived in Perth. A couple times a year she sends her brother dried food packets by Misses Malay that takes two months to reach him. She rambled on telling me about her family for about three or four stops, then picked up her bag, smiled and waved as she exited the train.

Georgetown Penang, Malaysia

You can't visit Penang without taking in the colonial city of Georgetown, known as the culinary capital of Malaysia. We made our way to a recommended food gallery where I had my first laksa soup, a Malaysian coconut curry soup. The experience wouldn't have been complete without sitting on tiny little red stools, with our butt cheeks spilling over the sides.

It was an assault on the senses. The aroma of roasted duck floated by accompanied by the scrape of spatulas on woks. There was a sea of humanity, from families with hoards of kids to young teens on dates. We were the only white faces in the throngs, except for the grey-haired guy in Birkenstocks and a flowered shirt playing the saxophone amidst the diners, which was quite an unexpected sight.

The array of food stalls seemed chaotic to us but everyone seemed to naturally flow through the haphazard aisles like a school of fish and join in the right queue ready to place their orders. As I looked around at the diners, some ate with their fingers, some with forks and others with chopsticks. So much for figuring out what proper etiquette was!

We spent the afternoon exploring the streets and alleyways of Georgetown by motorbike (as we normally do). At one point we decided to take a break and hopped off the scooter at one of the prolific hawker stands for some noodles and a Carlsberg. An old lady who looked tired and worn out, walked in. She was bent over and bow-legged, and her weathered face told of a difficult life. She scanned the busy establishment, spied us, shuffled over expressionless and pointed to the empty stool beside me.

I smiled and nodded. I thought I saw a brief sparkle in her eye.

Was she just looking to take a load off her feet or maybe for us to buy her lunch? She fingered her worn leather change purse and ordered a Milo (sort of like Nestle Quick chocolate milk). She sat there so serene, exuding a calmness that seeped into me. When she went to pay, it was in slow motion. She unzipped her change purse so methodically I could count each tooth as the pull-tab slid along the zipper. She dumped the contents onto the table . . . a few coins and one bill—10RM—the drink was two. She paid her bill and got up and left us without a word and without looking back.

The Smells of Penang

The lasting impressions I have of Penang, other than the curious assortment of people, was of cinnamon, cardamom, ginger & garlic, tinged with the aroma of stinky socks! I reassured myself that it was just the smell of durian fruit (which is banned in most high-end resorts). I did my best to ignore the brown, garbage-filled streams running through the storm drains that ran alongside shops and hawker stands. If you have never had a taste of durian fruit it's worth a try if you can get beyond the smell of it, stinky socks with a bit of cow patty or chicken coop thrown in.

Amazingly enough, putting it in your mouth actually cuts the sense of smell out immediately and engages the taste buds. It's a most unusual sensation. The flavour is a mild papaya like sensation with a similar texture but creamier and the fruit is wrapped around a large seed somewhat like a peach pit. Even with my dulled sense of smell, the almost pleasant flavour wouldn't entice me to try durian again any time soon. If I did, I would make sure I finished the whole thing in one sitting rather than carrying it around for any length of time to enjoy later. Once it's opened the smell lingers and will waft out of any bag or container it's being carried in and envelop its unwary carrier.

The cacophony of sites and sounds are all at once enveloping and assaulting. Unless you release yourself to it your nerves will be jangling like little brass cymbals all over your body. A little yoga breathing helped but making sure I was in a "good smell zone" before I deeply inhaled was important. A turning stomach added to jangling nerves is not the ideal recipe for a good time. Around each corner was a different smell so waiting for a good one (like lavender wafting out of one of the many spas along the way) became the mission.

During our explorations we found the botanical gardens where the sites, sounds and smells were all pleasant. A deep inhalation at any point rewarded the olfactory senses with a mix of rose, evergreen and eucalyptus. There was flora I had never seen before like tiny, blue ferns and oak leaves as big as me. When I picked up one and stood the stem on the ground, the top of the leaf reached almost to the top of my head!

During this Malaysian adventure, we also did a short hop to Tioman Island. It's the perfect place for a quiet get away . . . I mean really quiet and naturally beautiful. They keep it that way by not allowing any cars on the island, only golf carts. We stayed at Berjaya Resort and it was recommended we do the 2.5 km walk to the turtle sanctuary. We're big nature lovers and always up for a hike so off we went.

I've never seen so many shades of green as we meandered slowly along the trail, inhaling the wafts of breeze that carried the scent of wildflowers. The mountains on one side were walls of foliage of every shape and size. There were more of those leaves as big as me standing end to end. Part way along the walk was very long and narrow, with an 18-hole golf course on the ocean side. We spoke briefly to a couple from Scotland who were playing and said they had never lost so many balls. The only other human being we saw along the way was a security guard stationed outside a deserted vacation club (time share) perched on the side of the mountain overlooking the sea. There were other primates though. We were curiously followed along our walk by a band of monkeys. They stuck to the trees, of course. An assortment of bright yellow, fluorescent turquoise and jet-black butterflies completed our entourage. Now I know what has inspired various shades of colour: forest green (but which one), moss green, emerald green (but did that originate with the gem?), blue/green or maybe turquoise.

CHAPTER 15

Petra, Jordan – Rescued by a Bedouin

It was while trekking to the ancient city of Petra in Jordan that I was sure I heard voices. They started very quietly as we made our way through the long and narrow, mile-long ravine known as the Siq, that leads into the city. The walls almost reverberated with the whispered stories of those who had lived and visited there over the centuries.

I smiled, congratulating myself on my over active imagination, or maybe it was a bit of a sixth sense. Either way, I allowed myself to get swept up in the mystical feeling that washed over me as I absorbed my surroundings, flanked by spectacularly high mountains of rock from which the Siq was carved 2000 years ago. The layered colours reminded me of a muted Neapolitan ice cream with swirls of soft peach, liquorish, caramel and cream. The tranquillity was periodically broken by the clatter of hooves as horses and donkeys passed by bringing tourists into this hidden settlement in the mountains.

We had declined the ride, preferring to take advantage of the exercise the mile-long stroll afforded. The pathway spilled us onto a plaza that felt like a Hollywood movie set, which it was in "Indiana Jones and the Last Crusade" with Harrison Ford. I stopped and looked up, way up, at the first building you see as you enter Petra. There in front of me, the 40 by 30 metre façade, in all its hand-carved majesty, was the Pharoah's Treasury. I recognized it from one of the scenes in the film. Standing there, right in front of it, I could feel the energy of the buying and selling of wares of a time long ago. Maybe I was just remembering Indiana Jones and the guy dressed in black with the big sword but I think I have his adventures confused. It wasn't quite as frantic as I imagined the marketplace of a bygone era, but there were still a few local Bedouins plying their trade from wooden kiosks, a camel or two parked at each one.

It was definitely a step back in time and the locals, a few who still live right in Petra and others who have moved out into government-built housing, still hawk their wares to the hundreds of thousands of tourists who visit each year.

We discovered the biggest moneymaker for them was the "taxis" that take you to the most popular sites in the settlement. Some are a horrendous trek to get to and take time, stamina and lots of water to reach. To save wear and tear on feet and body, you can choose from a variety of taxis: horse, donkey or camel. The most comfortable option is the horse that pulls a carriage-style cart but it can't reach some of the more out of the way spots. So, the majority choose the donkey that can get to the highest places, through the narrowest pathways and up the steepest inclines. We were told it could be a bit hair-raising via donkey, so we decided to bite the bullet and go on foot.

Getting to the High Place of Sacrifice was a challenging hike straight up. Occasionally a breath of air would break through the dense humidity, whispering encouragement. I forged ahead. It was well worth the agony as the reward was the most coveted view of the day. Overlooking the Street of Facades in the distance, I imagined the religious ceremonies that were held in this sacred place that honoured the Nabataean Gods. It had also been the site used for funeral rites.

Undaunted after the exhausting yet successful hike to the High Place, we pushed onward, eager to see the Monastery. It was an 800-stair journey, during which I tried to ignore the burning in my shins and focus on the breath-taking rainbow sandstone mountains. I was glad we took the advice of the hotel owner to wait until the sun had dipped below the mountain before making this trek and also to bring lots of water.

I paused often, seemingly to enjoy the scenery but in actuality, I found it a tough slog. I insisted that my travel companion go ahead and we would meet at the monastery. Halfway up I accepted a cup of very sugary tea from a local Bedouin woman tucked into a crevice in the side of the mountain off one of the steps. She was selling an odd assortment of old jewellery covered in dust, from camel bone necklaces to ancient amulets dug up in the ruins (so I was told).

"Sit, have tea," she beckoned to me and pointed to her small, rickety table. I knew she would try to sell me something but my companion who was way ahead of me had the money. I shook my head but paused to catch my breath. I could feel my face pounding and imagined the crimson colour it must have been.

"Sit," she insisted. "No sell."

So, I sat and thankfully accepted the cup she offered with a smile and a nod. It was then I noticed a tiny figure peacefully asleep under the table.

"Your baby?" I asked pointing to the slumbering tot.

"My . . . yes," she put her hand over her heart and smiled. Tears filled her eyes.

She told me her story in Arabic, but it was

peppered with enough English words that I got the gist of it. Her husband was gone. I couldn't quite catch why or where, but it still meant that she was alone raising her child. I felt helpless. I wanted to give her something but what?

I sat with her for a long while, just listening and holding her hand while she cried. She finally wiped her tears on the sleeve of her black cloak. She reached over to the table and picked up one of the camel bone necklaces and held it out to me.

I got up and dusted myself off. "No, I'm sorry," I said. "I have no money." I felt terrible. I had drank her tea and kept her from engaging with several tourists who laboured past us up the steep stairway. They were certainly going slow enough to be the perfect targets.

"No money," she said, pressed the necklace into my hand and squeezed it. "Shukran." She whispered.

Thank-you? It was one of the few Arabic words I knew. I was speechless. It appeared all she wanted was for someone to listen to her story.

I had read that many of these women still lived the nomadic lifestyle of their ancestors where storytelling is a much-loved pastime. They made their homes in the mountains in tents in the winter and in the caves, which are cooler, in the summer. The tents were much further up in the mountains and only the most intrepid explorer would get a glimpse. Would we be so lucky?

The sugary tea and the treasured gift I wore around my neck had restored my energy, so I continued up the stairs. As I reached the top, there was a wide expanse of rocks, pebbles and sand, with several rugged little shops and kiosks around the perimeter but on the other side, the grandeur of the monastery rose like Goliath and snatched the remaining air from my lungs. I took a few deep breaths and absorbed the energy of my new surroundings.

I scanned the area and spotted my companion in the entrance to a cave directly behind me, where a canteen was set up inside. It had big loungers with cushions where you could sprawl out, sip a cold drink and gaze at the monastery and imagine the time it took to carve just the entrance alone with the rudimentary tools of 300 BC. It stood several stories high. I took full advantage of the cool respite after our long trek reading more about this lost civilization.

The return was a bit easier but we still took our time. My Bedouin angel was not at her post, which was disappointing, as I wanted to buy something from her. *Maybe I'd see her tomorrow*, I thought to myself. A gust of wind kicked up and blew a small dust devil that swirled around my legs. The wind ricocheted off the rock wall and bounced back,

"*Inshallah*," (God willing), it whispered. I shook my head. I was hearing things.

• • •

We had made it back to the hotel just before the heavens opened. It was such torrential rain that we opted to stay in and eat family style with our host, Yusef. It was a lively evening with an impromptu serenading by the hotel owner and a few local friends. By morning the rains had let up and as we pored over the tourist maps and guides, Yusef sidled up to us conspiratorially and winked.

"You look like you might be up for a bit more of a challenge today," he grinned.

I was about to deny his statement, thinking about the cramps in my calves the night before but before I could stop myself the adventurer in me chimed in.

"Sure, what would you suggest?"

The voice in my head wasn't whispering, it was shouting *Tell him no*! But I knew it was probably the only time I would be in Jordan so I smiled, encouraging him to continue. My mother always said you can sleep when you're dead!

"Well, when you come to the entryway for the Siq, there's a small shack where you can hire a donkey," he began.

I knew exactly where he meant as we had seen it the day before.

"Right behind the shack is an unmarked path that is difficult to see as it's very narrow and sort of covered with brush. It's not an 'official' pathway so few people use it. But the hike is spectacular. You see many beautiful things."

"Where does it go?" I ventured; my curiosity had definitely gotten the better of me.

"It cuts through the mountain on the opposite side to the Siq and then comes out at the Street of Facades."

"How long?" I started packing up the map. I knew then that we were going the road less travelled.

"Oh, maybe two, three hours," he waved his hand in the air. "Not long."

Considering we had hiked a full nine hours the day before (minus the 10-minute donkey ride we gave in to on the very last leg back through the Siq), this sounded like a piece of cake. We'd be back for lunch! Or, so I thought.

It started out gangbusters. We found the pathway Yusef talked about right away and took to it like a baby to its first taste of chocolate pudding. We soon approached a narrowing in the path, and a group of people were heading towards us.

"It doesn't look safe," said a man at the front of the group. "I don't think it's passable."

"Thanks," I said as we continued past them. "We'll see how far we get."

They were the last people we saw on the path that day. As I watched them disappear through the bramble that led back to the main path a gust of wind lifted my hat from my head and tossed it back in the direction we came. I retrieved it as the gust followed me and danced around my ears. I was distracted. I should have listened to the wind but all I could think of was the adventure waiting to be had.

Passable is definitely a relative term. It all depends on how much scooching, crawling, squeezing, balancing, climbing and scrambling you're up for. We were in 'exploration' mode so anything that didn't seem life threatening, albeit uncomfortable, didn't hold us back. At one point, we were almost horizontal, with hands on one wall and feet on another as we scooched along, attempting to keep our feet dry from the small river that flowed between the narrow walls. One misstep later and I was lying in the muddy water. I laughed as I stood up in the ankle-deep stream and sloshed towards a dry ledge at the end. I was wet, but not hurt. On the other side, the path was dry and it widened nicely. We were rewarded with even more spectacular views.

The landscape was dotted with purple and pink desert flowers and spiky cacti. I was again in awe of the mountains surrounding us. As we progressed along the pathway it widened and narrowed every hundred yards or so in between sheer rock faces decorated with a cacophony of patterns. My camera snapped away at the chaotic swirls belaying a history of tumultuous weather with layers of carbon, marble and clay each denoting a new century. The perfect circles juxtaposed with jagged lines creating tapestries suitable for any art gallery wall. It was modern abstract, yet ancient art all at the same time.

We kept trekking and marvelling, not really taking note of the time until we came to a halt as the path had widened and then dipped into what appeared to be a small lake that totally blocked the way. It was about a half mile across and then the path obviously took an upturn and dry land resumed. There was no way around it as it lapped against the walls of the mountains on either side.

"How deep can it be?" I wondered out loud. We could both swim but I wasn't sure I wanted to find out. "Maybe we can climb up and go around it."

But, the cliffs were sheer and we didn't bring our rappelling ropes I joked. We had never done any real rock climbing before and with my fear of heights it wasn't on my 'to do' list.

I was getting desperate as we were running out of ideas. I looked at my watch and it was already three o'clock. I didn't think it was a good idea to turn back. We wouldn't make it out before dark.

I couldn't believe we had already been hiking six hours. The mud and other 'water hazards' had probably slowed us down. It dawned on me that when Yusef recommended the alternate pathway, he had forgotten how much rain had fallen lately.

"Look there. It looks like a Bedouin." I pointed way above to a tiny, turbaned, old man who was waving furiously at us and pointing to the water. He shook his head and then held up his hand like he wanted us to stop. Then he disappeared.

A breeze rustled the thorny bush behind me and the nettles rubbed against the rock. *Sssstaaay*, it whispered.

We heard a scrabbling and looked behind us and up. The little old man was lowering himself down to a small ledge, probably not much wider than the length of my foot. He braced himself and took the black rope that was wrapped around his head holding his white turban in place. He lowered it down towards us and he pointed to me and motioned for me to climb up.

"Here, let me give you a leg up," my companion crouched down and clasped his hands together with the palms up creating a step.

I took a deep breath, put one foot in the cradle of his hands and heaved up to grab the rope. With a little pushing and the little man pulling, I made it to the ledge, heart pounding in my throat.

The little man made the same cradle with his hands and looked up. I wasn't sure I would be able to reach the top but spending the night in the gulley with more rain coming didn't really appeal to me so I took a deep breath and placed my foot in his hands. My other foot slipped and just as I was losing my balance, he gave a great heave and shot me up with a strength I wouldn't have believed if I hadn't felt it myself. I was catapulted up and onto solid ground at the top of the cliff.

I did a few tumbles and by the time I had gathered my wits about me and scrambled back to the edge and looked down, my companion was on the ledge ready for his ride. I backed away and prayed. He weighed a lot more than me and I was doubtful that the little Bedouin man could manage the same miracle with him. I almost shouted down that I would go for help when my companion tumbled over the edge and seconds later, our rescuer hopped up beside him.

My first impulse was to wrap my arms around him in a big bear hug but I stopped myself in time. I was in a Muslim country and it would be horrifying for him if I did that. I clamped my hands in front of my chest in prayer and bobbed my head up and down frantically so he would know just how much we appreciated his help. That was when I noticed that he was not more than five feet tall. What was even more amazing was that on his feet was a pair of dusty, holey, black dress shoes. How he accomplished the feat of saving our asses is beyond me but we lived to tell the tale.

He sheepishly reached into his pocket and brought out a handful of old coins.

He wanted to sell us something.

"Whatever he's selling, I'm buying!" I looked at his offering and amidst the coins was an identical amulet as my other Bedouin angel had on her table of treasures. It was battered and worn and one of the turquoise stones was missing. I picked it up and held it in my hand. I could almost feel the energy pulsing from it.

"How much for this and this," I picked one of the old coins from his hand adding it to the amulet in mine.

"Three dinar," he said softly.

I nodded and handed our rescuer the money, the equivalent of which was $US5.

A soft breeze kicked up the dust and ruffled the brim of my hat. *Safe* was the whisper I heard. The voice was right. We were going to be just fine as we recognized the Street of Facades in the distance that would lead us to the exit and home.

We turned back to thank our rescuer again, but he had disappeared into the hills.

My little amulet will always remind me to listen

to the voices. But then again, if I had, I wouldn't have the story of being rescued by a Bedouin.

CHAPTER 16

South Africa – Kapama Game Park

The African safari is a dream vacation for the adventurer, the naturalist, the eco-tourist and photographer looking for the "Big 5." I fancied myself all of the above as we launched out on our African adventure!

Safari travel to South Africa often begins by flying into Johannesburg. Those more adventurous travellers that opt to pass on the organized tours and strike out on their own will often rent a car from there, and that's exactly what we did. We had a brief moment of panic when we left the airport in our rental car. It was late at night and we really didn't have a clue where we were going. In our haste, we neglected to consult the map before we got on the road. The exit signs were so confusing that we finally pulled over and spread the map out on the dashboard, always a big no-no when traveling in a strange country. I glanced in the side view mirror and saw a group of about six guys approaching from behind. I suggested a quick exit and just as we started the car and put it into drive, they had split up and were flanking us on both sides. We had done exactly what our South African friends had told us not to do . . . stop anywhere after dark! Well, luckily, we got away and lived to tell the tale.

The drive to Kapama Game Reserve, one of South Africa's popular game parks, takes about eight hours from Jo-Burg. My South African friends had suggested that we make a couple of stops on the way.

We took their advice and after a leisurely three-hour drive northbound from the Johannesburg Airport we found a cute little town called Dullstrom. It is said to have the best views in the high veldt, and a great place to take a break and stop for a little fly-fishing. Who could resist?

We found a lodge called Millstream Farm that stocked trout in their small ponds that were dotted amongst the lush green hills of the property. The pathways were also frequented by an assortment of spring bok. It was there that I had my first sighting. I was so excited I almost peed myself, and we weren't even on safari yet! After a quick fly-fishing lesson in the rain, I caught my very first trout. Rain, fog and trout. I felt like I was back home in Nova Scotia.

The next morning, we continued our drive through the mountains with a stop for lunch overlooking Blyde River Canyon and on into Nelspruitt town where we decided to stay another night at a local bed & breakfast. There were so many to choose from but the one with the most spectacular view of the mountains was La Roca Guest House, which featured a gorgeous Eggs Benedict over local smoked trout for breakfast.

After an early breakfast, we left for Kapama Game Reserve, located on the southern edge of Kruger National Park. It was just a short two-hour drive from Nelspruitt. Kruger Park is 20,000 square kilometres of protected wildlife preserve on the border of Mozambique. Visitors can drive themselves through Kruger Park but a private safari lodge often offers a closer look into the natural habitat of the African wildlife.

Kapama had several different accommodation options from the elegant River Lodge overlooking the reserve to individual chalets. We chose the more adventurous option, the tents of the Buffalo Camp on stilts in the very heart of the park where we would have 24/7 contact with the animals in addition to two game drives a day.

Our guide picked us up at the safari lodge and escorted us to the interior of the bush veldt where our tent awaited. This wasn't any ordinary tent though. It was luxury! It sat way up on a platform on stilts and the tent flap where you normally unzip and climb in, was actually a sliding glass door. The only similarity to the tents we were used to is that it was made of canvas and nylon. As we entered our accommodation, the first thing I noticed was a full queen-size bed. I then spied the en suite bathroom that not only had a sink with hot and cold running water, but also a stand-up shower as well, big enough for two! This was my kind of camping.

We barely caught our breath when we were reminded that our ranger and tracker were waiting to lead us on our first sunset safari. So, we grabbed our welcome drinks and boarded an open-air Land Rover with stadium seating so all could have an unobstructed view from any seat. It didn't really matter, as we were the only ones on the drive that night.

The first day we saw the most common sights - buffalo, wart hogs and guinea fowls. A good tracker will eventually find the herds of giraffe, zebra and elephant, which ours did as he sat perched on a tiny little platform that jutted out from the hood of the jeep. He was hopeful that we might be part of the lucky few get a glimpse of the nocturnal leopard. I thought I caught a flash of leopard print dashing through the trees at one point but, alas, it was just a large spotted ganet.

Our guide who drove the jeep was terrific! When he realized what nature buffs we were he even pointed out the smaller creatures like chameleons and even dung beetles, which totally mesmerized me.

At Buffalo Camp, we were treated to four-course, gourmet meals served by the ranger (the small staff at the camp wore many hats which minimizes the impact too many people can have on the natural environment). The camp only accommodates 16 guests at a time. The rangers also doubled as bartenders as we finished our meals and meandered over to the lounge for a nightcap.

Each night we retired early as the wake-up call for the morning game drive came at five a.m. It's the best time to capture the animals on film as they start their day before the heat of midday when they hide from view in the shade of the bush to keep cool.

The daily game drives were scheduled for six a.m. and four p.m., so the recommended midday entertainment was to take in the Cheetah Research Centre close by. The centre takes care of injured cheetahs as well as other animals that have been mistreated in zoos or circuses. The ultimate goal is to reintroduce them into the wild but those that have had too much human contact have to remain at the centre, as they wouldn't have the ability to fend for themselves in the wild.

All in all, an incredible trip, with tons of memories and fantastic photos! If you'd like to check out the game park we visited, here's the website: www.kapama.co.za.

CHAPTER 17

The Floating Islands of Peru

When most travellers decide to go to Peru, the focal point of the trip is usually to visit the ancient ruins of Macchu Picchu. It's a must-see on any adventure traveller's agenda but the Uros Floating Islands of Peru are worth a look as well. More than 40 of these unique floating islands can be found on Lake Titicaca, the highest navigable lake in the world some 12,000 feet above sea level, and also South America's largest lake. Located in the Southeastern part of Peru the closest city is Puno. The far side of the lake is bordered by Bolivia.

Flying into the nearest airport in Juliaca is possible but the more intrepid traveller may choose to explore the country more intensely by flying into Lima and then taking several days and various modes of transportation to truly experience the flavour of the countryside, the people and the culture.

Following the winding narrow roads of Peru into

the mountains and into the small town of Puno, so high above sea level almost touching the clouds, the spectacular expanse of Lake Titicaca that greets visitors rounding the corner coming out of town is postcard perfect. There's not much to see in Puno so most travellers head straight to the lake to the floating islands nestled amongst the natural islands of Taquile and Amantani. None of the islands, natural or man-made, have any cars or roads, only footpaths and peace and tranquillity. The lake is a very spiritual place, as it is believed that Manco Capac, the original Incan chieftain, rose from the waters of Lake Titicaca to create the Incan Empire.

The floating islands are made by hand from tortora reeds by the Quechua and Aymara Indians that inhabit the islands and welcome visitors, even for overnight stays so they can experience the simple lifestyle of the natives. The amenities are limited. However, there is the odd hut sporting a satellite dish precariously perched atop its thatched roof along with solar panels to power the rare television. The same type of reed is also used to make the island dwellers' homes and boats. Reed boats take travellers from one floating island to the next with a special visit to the main island where the schoolhouse sits.

Wrap up the visit on the lake with lunch on Taquile where the only footpath leads visitors on a steep journey through Incan and pre-Incan stone ruins and terraced farms into town where the local children adorn newcomers with friendship bracelets they've woven by hand, which are said to bring good luck. Plans should be made in advance as, with enough warning, lunch is typically prepared and served in one of the locals' homes. There are a few very simple restaurants near the central plaza but the home-cooked meal and hospitality is the favoured experience.

Best times to visit are February or November when the Semana de Puno festivities celebrating the Incan culture are in full swing and Peruvian folklore is celebrated.

Eating in Peru

A stop along the way to sample the popular cuy that is common on Peruvian menus could be on the agenda (but not for the faint of heart or travellers with more delicate sensibilities as this delicacy is actually guinea pig). Most locals don't know the English term so an understandable translation when trying to determine the type of meat in the dish is not usually forthcoming.

CHAPTER 18

Bare Boating BVI Style

The rope bit into the soft flesh from the pressure of my grip. With teeth clenched and eyes shut, I could imagine the bow of thirty-two and a half feet of lean sailing machine ripping through the icy waves as I fought to tighten the jib. I felt the punch of the wind as it filled the mainsail and we lunged forward. My maiden voyage had begun.

With the first tack successfully completed I cautiously loosened my grip and slowly opened one eye, then the other. Stretching for miles ahead was a glittering, turquoise playground inviting us to chart our course into a real-life paradise known as the British Virgin Islands or B.V.I. I heaved a sigh of relief, gave a thumbs-up to my skipper and sat back to enjoy my first sailing experience, à la bareboat.

Our "bare" sailboat was a Beneteau 325, chartered from The Moorings on the Island of Tortola and fully equipped with everything but a crew. Boats range in size from 32-60 feet and can accommodate from 2-10 people.

The term bare boating refers to what you have to bring with you to outfit the boat, which is nothing. It also means you sail it yourself. However, they will provide a skipper if there is no one in your party who can fit the bill. The charter company will provision the boat with all you need; even a barbeque. Just bring yourself and very little clothing, (it can get very hot!).

Once aboard our floating hotel, (which was home for five days and nights), the two of us set sail to live out our wildest dreams!

Our days were filled with adventures too numerous to list. From playing castaways on the uninhabited shores of Eustatia Island to lazily sipping rum punch at Rhymer's Beach Bar and restaurant in Cane Garden Bay. Swimming, snorkelling, hiking, fishing and sailing, (of course), were also part of the B.V.I. experience.

The bare boating experience appeals to a wide variety of people. For beginner sailors, it is very comforting never to be out of sight of land, yet for the experienced sailor, there are still plenty of opportunities to test navigational skills.

The charter company will provide you with the necessary navigational charts but you are responsible for charting your own course. If you need help, they are more than happy to make suggestions. You should also bring along a cruising guide to the Virgin Islands to help plan your day trips and nightly anchorages.

First published in Canadian Airlines *inflight magazine, December 1992. Canadian Airlines officially merged with Air Canada in January 2001.*

CHAPTER 19

Sailing the Greek Isles

Eight close friends, a country steeped in history, warm breezes, and a 51-foot sailboat is my recipe for a wonderfully exotic and exciting adventure.

The planning and anticipation are always half the fun—and the planning usually pays off!

Before we even boarded our 'floating hotel' for our bareboat sail one of the newest of our group stated, "You've already exceeded my expectations." We had just spent our second glorious day on the beautiful island of Santorini, a brief stop before picking up our boat on the island of Naxos. We took a scooter tour of the island which ended at the rustic, traditional Santos Winery on top of a cliff in the town of Akrotiri—the sunset was spectacular and a wedding ceremony overlooking the valley was taking place.

In the Greek Islands, there is no shortage of beautiful places that are just perfect for the wedding of your dreams. Santorini would definitely get my vote. When exploring the Greek Islands, Santorini is a must, but it is tricky for boaters as the port is deep and anchoring is difficult. Taking a ferry to this island, as we did, is strongly recommended.

Sadly, we left the breath-taking island of Santorini yet eager to trade our scooters for another mode of transportation—the sailboat that would be our home for the next week.

And a bareboat sailing holiday is the ultimate escape. The term 'bareboat' means that you charter a boat and sail it yourself. If there isn't a skipper in your group of friends, you can easily hire one.

The next stop for us was the island of Naxos where we boarded our 51-foot Jeanneau sailboat—aptly named 'Carpe Diem'—and prepared to 'seize the day'.

The first order of the day was to shop for provisions for the week at a local market just a few feet from the dock. If you really want to be spoiled, you can hire a cook to travel with you too. Most well-appointed charter sailboats have crew quarters on board for such a situation. However, the food in Greece is so good and so reasonable you'll probably find that hiring a cook isn't necessary. Most restaurants are family owned and operated and the minute you walk in the door, you're treated as a member of the family—and the best way to really enjoy the warm hospitality of the Greek people is to have a meal with them.

Our choice was to just stock up with traditional Greek delicacies—slabs of fresh feta cheese, vegetables grown in a garden we could see just outside the back door, and garlic-laden tzatziki. After shopping we settled down to a 'welcome to Naxos' ouzo at Yanni's where we were joined by a group of local sponge fishermen along with Yanni's entire family! Another Greek feast and an evening of live entertainment—complete with an impromptu demonstration of a traditional Greek dance—topped off our day.

The next day began another chapter of our Greet Isles storybook holiday.

There are thousands of Greek islands (not all inhabited) and one is more beautiful than the next. Having a loose itinerary is a good idea or you could spend your whole vacation getting from one island to another. Our plan was to stick to what's known as the Cyclades Islands in the Aegean Sea. This body of water separates Greece and Turkey and is just north of the Sea of Crete. It's always a good plan to pack a local guidebook for some suggested itineraries and helpful hints. The one I chose was *Greece: The Cyclades* by Dana Facaros. It's part of the Cadogen Island Guides series and was very helpful. Fodor's guides are also thorough and entertaining.

One of the most amazing things about Greece is its history, both real and mythological. In ancient times, the Greeks believed that all events that occurred were actions of the Gods. When traveling the Greek Islands, there were stories of how each island was formed by one God or another, with mountains erupting as battles were waged. Keeping track of historical and mythological events relating to each island we visited was both educational and intriguing.

Once such island was Sifnos. Snuggled between Serifos and Paros, Sifnos has a charm and history you can feel as you slowly motor into the peaceful cove of Faros. Mythology tells of the Sifnioted mining gold (which was plentiful on the island in 530 BC) and bringing it up into the mountains as an offering to the God Apollo. When looking up the sheer Cliffside, the ruins of an ancient castle can be seen and above the castle, the island's most famous church, Panayia Chrissopigi.

Both are an easy hike from the anchorage, up a narrow donkey-path that starts at the beach known as Fasolou. We decided to take advantage of the opportunity for some exercise, and once we arrived at the top of the mountain were rewarded with a panoramic view that would make your heart sing.

But then, breath-taking views are the norm on the Greek Islands. Greece has always been an artist's paradise. However, artists are not the only ones who have been attracted to these gems of the Aegean. Colourful characters entered our picture book adventure at every turn. From the salty sponge divers on Naxos, to the cosmopolitan couple (he from Athens and she from Holland) who welcomed us to their taverna overlooking the beach in Faros.

The best part of a Greek Islands bare boating adventure is the variety of activities. For the less adventurous looking for peaceful contemplation, the miles of white sandy beach on Ios is perfect to settle in with a good book—while the daredevils can head into the hills for some hair-raising, dirt-biking. If shopping is your passion, most of the islands have wonderful collections of boutiques and shops you can visit as you wind your way through narrow, cobble-stoned streets, surrounded by pristine, whitewashed buildings adorned with blue shutters and doors.

In our travels we found the best islands for shopping, nightlife and action were Mykonos, Santorini, Naxos, Paros and Ios. The smaller, less developed islands were best for peaceful days of hiking and quiet soul-searching. Many travellers whose paths we crossed were exploring the islands by way of ferry. If you're not a sailor, this is an easy and enjoyable way to see several islands in one trip.

We ended our adventure on the island of Paros

where we packed our bags and handed Carpe Diem back to her owner. One final dinner in a cozy taverna and one more stroll through the winding Grecian streets completed this chapter of our exotic Greek Island adventure.

First published in Panache *magazine, Sarasota, FL, January 2000.*

CHAPTER 20

Exploring the Greek Island of Hydra

It would take years to sail all of the Greek Islands but each one has such a unique personality, choosing ones that fit a particular taste is easy.

There are thousands of islands between the coasts of Greece and Turkey in the Aegean Sea, the Mediterranean Sea and the Sea of Crete but only a little over 200 are inhabited. In ancient times, some of the uninhabited islands were off limits to mere mortals after dark, as it was believed that the Gods came down from the heavens and stayed on islands such as Delos in the Cyclades Island group.

Popular Greek Islands

The busy tourist islands of Mykonos and Santorini, also located in the Cyclades, are popular with travellers looking for shopping and busy main port activity, however many smaller islands, like the island of Hydra (or Idhra) located to the west in the Peloponnese, will attract those more interested in going back in time.

Hydra Island

The island has no cars, and residents get around on donkey or by foot. Most restaurants grow their own vegetables, as importing fresh produce is a pricey endeavour. The only way to get to Hydra is by ferry or private boat and it's a popular destination for sailors looking for some peace.

Arriving at Hydra Port

Privately owned and chartered sailboats and motorboats arriving at Hydra are escorted into the anchorage by a self-appointed harbour master named Popeye, a colourful character who carefully guides vessels into the tightly packed area. In high season, many boats are moored together, end-to-end with the first one to arrive tied to the town quay by the stern with an anchor set from the bow. It's advised to arrive early but be ready to stay late into the following day while waiting for others to depart and while Popeye assists in untangling the anchor lines that inevitably get crossed in the melee.

Hydra's History

For a tiny island its history is renowned. In the 1800s the admiral of the Greek fleet was from Hydra and according to the Greek Waters Pilot, "but for the Hydrio fleet and sailors, the War of Independence would not have been won." However, following the war the memory faded and the island was ignored until travellers re-discovered its charm in later years and it began attracting artists and writers and those looking for an escape.

Hydra Today

Even as its popularity grows, Hydra seems to have paused in the 18th century. Most of the waterfront houses were built between 1770 and 1821 and are now on the list of Europe's protected monuments. The narrow cobblestone road that leads from the port into Hydra town is a study in architectural history, interspersed with shops selling everything from hand made arts & crafts to jewellery.

A big draw on all the Greek Islands, and Hydra is no exception, is the welcoming, family-friendly tavernas and restaurants that boast homemade Greek dishes. The meals are usually accompanied by the famous Retsina wine, unique to Greece, and then typically finished off with a glass of ouzo while someone who looks like Zorba the Greek entertains the crowd with a traditional dance.

CHAPTER 21

Sailing St. Lucia to Martinique

Hectic schedules and formal dining aren't everybody's favourite way to see the Caribbean Islands. Some prefer a more intimate way to be immersed in the sun, sea and sand.

Chartering a sailboat can be a very exciting and gratifying experience. The sail from St. Lucia to Martinique, (the largest of the Windward Islands), provides a challenge for both the well-seasoned and the novice sailor.

Located between St. Vincent and Martinique, St. Lucia has some of the most breath-taking scenery and exhilarating sailing in the Caribbean. Coupled with the warm hospitality of the English-speaking residents and an ideal year-round tropical climate, St. Lucia is the perfect place to start a bareboat cruise.

There are several charter bases on the island and the tranquil blue lagoon of Marigot Bay, (on the Northwest coast of St. Lucia), is a good place to start.

When chartering a sailboat most companies can have the galley fully stocked upon arrival with a combination of familiar treats and an intriguing and colourful selection of local fruits and vegetables. Once everything is stowed and a reconnoitre of the surrounding area and familiarization of the boat is complete, the adventure continues!

The natural wonders of the island of St. Lucia come alive at Soufriere Bay. At dusk, watch the twin volcanic peaks of the Pitons embrace the last rays of sunshine as the native boat boys welcome visitors, coming alongside offering a rope to tie off on a palm tree ashore. Fresh coconut, mango and papaya are sold from floating boutiques along with beautiful, hand-made jewellery, fashioned from mahogany beans and bamboo shoots.

After a long day of sailing, a swim off the back of the boat is both refreshing and invigorating. Then a dinghy-ride ashore to investigate the catch of the day could net a sampling of some fresh conch. The locals are happy to demonstrate the fine art of extricating them from their shells.

The best place to make a final stop on the journey north along the coast of St. Lucia before the open water sail to Martinique is the cozy anchorage of Rodney Bay.

The crossing to Martinique is a thirty-three mile adventure accompanied by schools of flying fish and dolphins, amid rolling swells and strong but steady trade winds. Upon entering the busy port of Fort de France, you can feel the pulse of a busy city just waiting to be discovered.

It is worth the trip ashore to explore Fort de France, the largest city of the Windward Islands. The European influence on this French colony is reflected in narrow streets and colourful markets, where sailors can re-stock the pantry and barter for treasures to bring home.

Some choose to escape the hustle and bustle and explore the island by scooter. Hidden behind Fort de France's metropolitan mask is a cascade of lush green foliage and vibrant blossoms. A leisurely trek up the mountain to the Pitons du Carbet rewards visitors with the most beautiful vista.

From this mountain perch the shimmering white beaches that line the east coast of the island are in full view. The water is warm, crystal clear and inviting; a perfect spot to stop and do some windsurfing or snorkelling before heading back.

St. Lucia and Martinique are an adventurers' playground steeped in history and natural beauty. Diving shipwrecks from 1902 and exploring the tropical rain forests of St. Lucia, are all possible when cruising the "bareboat" way.

ABOUT THE AUTHOR

Anne Louise O'Connell grew up in Halifax, Nova Scotia and has lived around the world, escaping the cold of Canada on a hunt for warmer climes, with stops in Florida, Dubai and Thailand. In 2007, after 17 years in the PR business, O'Connell decided to focus on her real passion and just write. In 2016, she returned to her hometown and established OC Publishing.

O'Connell is a multi-genre author who has written both fiction and non-fiction. Her books include *Mental Pause*, her first novel that won an IPPY (*Independent Publisher* magazine) Book Award, and her second novel, *Deep Deceit*, the first in the Deep Mysteries series. Her first book was a non-fiction, *@Home in Dubai—Getting Connected Online and* *on the Ground.* She has also co-published a collaborative collection titled *Phuket Island Writers – An Anthology of Short Stories.*

O'Connell loves to mentor other authors, does developmental editing and assists others in their publishing journey and developing their author platforms. She enjoys editing and partner publishing women's fiction, historical fiction, mystery/suspense, memoir, YA, middle grade, and children's picture books. While she was living in Thailand, she was a contributing writer for *The Wall Street Journal* Expat Blog and *Global Living* magazine and a regular columnist for *Expat Focus*. She is also the creator and facilitator of the Paradise Writers' Retreat.

Connect with Anne:
Website: www.ocpublishing.ca
Facebook: www.facebook.com/ocpublishing
LinkedIn: www.linkedin.com/in/annelouiseoconnell
Instagram: ocpubhfx
Youtube.com/ocpublishing
TikTok: ocpubhfx

www.ingramcontent.com/pod-product-compliance
Lightning Source LLC
Chambersburg PA
CBHW030911080526
44589CB00010B/250